Death Valley

By Stephen Rickard

Published in 2026 by
Norwood House Press
2544 Clinton Street
Buffalo, NY 14224

Printed in the United States of America

Library of Congress Cataloging-in-Publication Data:
Names: Rickard, Stephen, 1957-, author. | Atkins, Jill (Children's author). | Muravski, Marie, illustrator.
Title: Death Valley / by Stepen Rickard. Helen Keller / written by Jill Atkins, illustrated by Marie Muravski.
Description: Buffalo, NY : Norwood House Press, 2026. | Series: Phonics all-stars: phase 5b
Identifiers: ISBN 9781978578265 (pbk.) | ISBN 9781978578272 (library bound) | ISBN 9781978578289 (ebook)
Subjects: LCSH: Reading–Phonetic method–Juvenile literature. | English language–Phonetics–Juvenile literature. | Death Valley (Calif. and Nev.)–Juvenile literature. | Keller, Helen, 1880-1968–Juvenile literature.
Classification: LCC LB1573.3 R534 2026 | DDC 372.465–dc23

CPSIA compliance information: Batch #CW26NHP: For further information contact Norwood House Press at 1-800-237-9932.

Death Valley sounds like the name of something in a computer game.

However, Death Valley exists! You can find it on a map, if you look at America.

In the summertime, Death Valley is the hottest point on the planet.

In 1913 it reached 134 degrees, which is the highest ever recorded.

There have been some whole years where Death Valley has seen no rain at all.

How did it get its name?

In 1849, at the time of the gold rush in America, a group of people were traveling across America in wagon trains, to reach the gold fields.

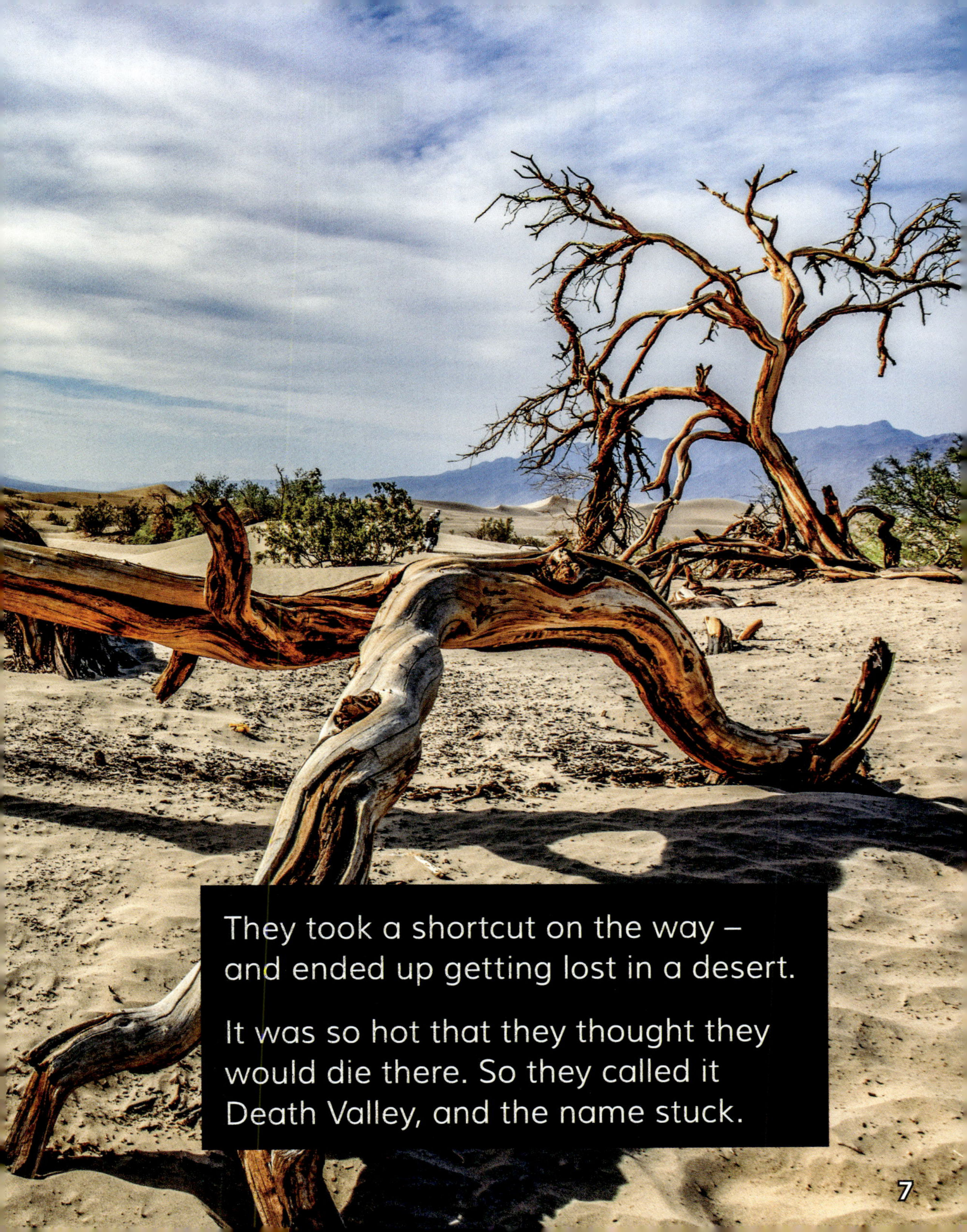

They took a shortcut on the way – and ended up getting lost in a desert.

It was so hot that they thought they would die there. So they called it Death Valley, and the name stuck.

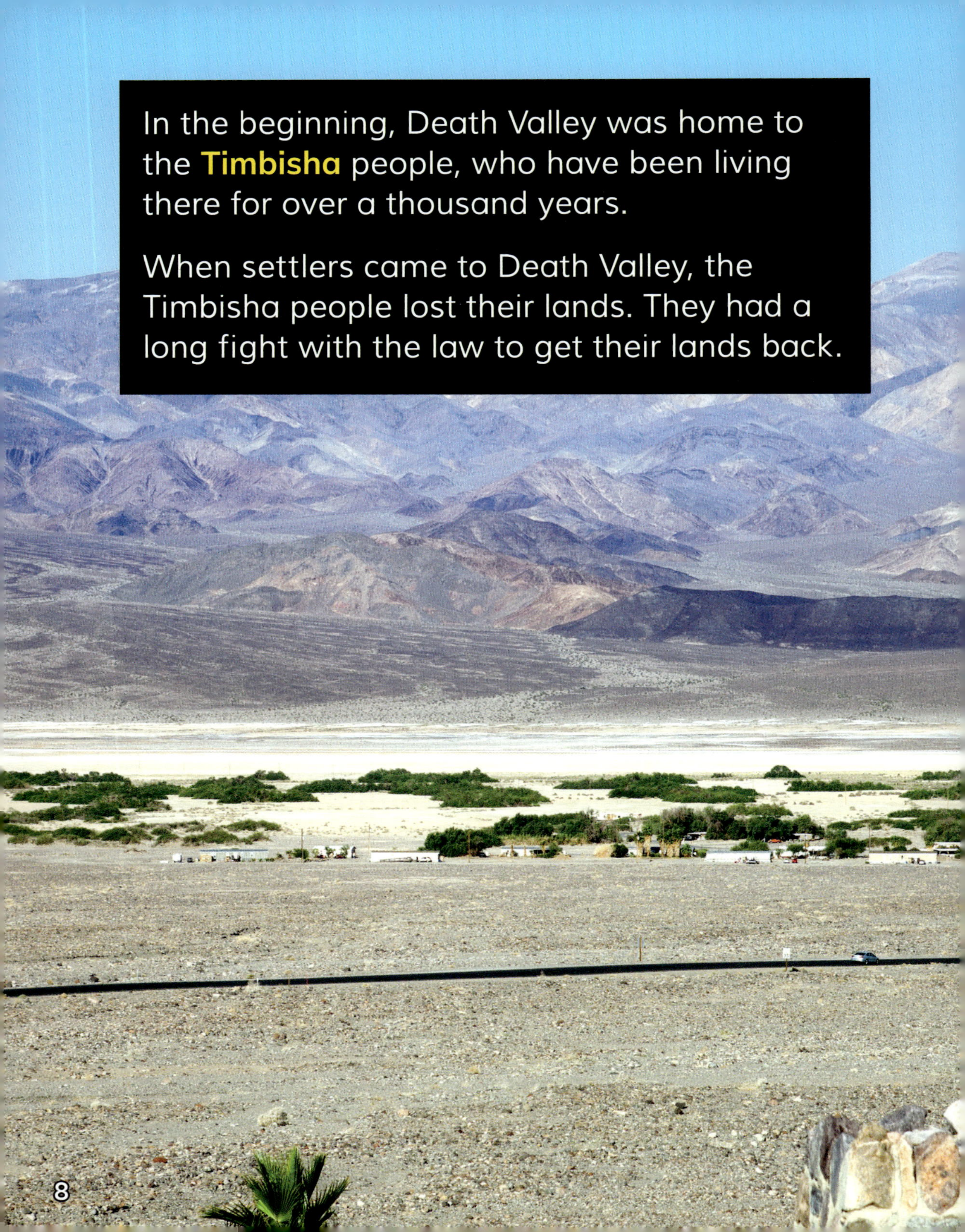

In the beginning, Death Valley was home to the **Timbisha** people, who have been living there for over a thousand years.

When settlers came to Death Valley, the Timbisha people lost their lands. They had a long fight with the law to get their lands back.

Some Timbisha families are still found in Death Valley today.

About 150 years ago, **borax** was found in Death Valley. (Borax is important to us – we use it for many different things.)

Borax mines were dug and many people traveled there to work in the mines.

A mule train in Death Valley, pulling wagons full of borax.

For a while, Death Valley was a boom town and it even had a railway.

Then, when the borax ran out, the mine was shut down.

Much of Death Valley is a big park.

You might think that it is so hot that no life can survive there, but that is not true.

As well as lots of different kinds of plants, you could meet sidewinder snakes, geckos, bobcats, and many kinds of lizards.

They all just keep out of the sun in the hottest part of the day!

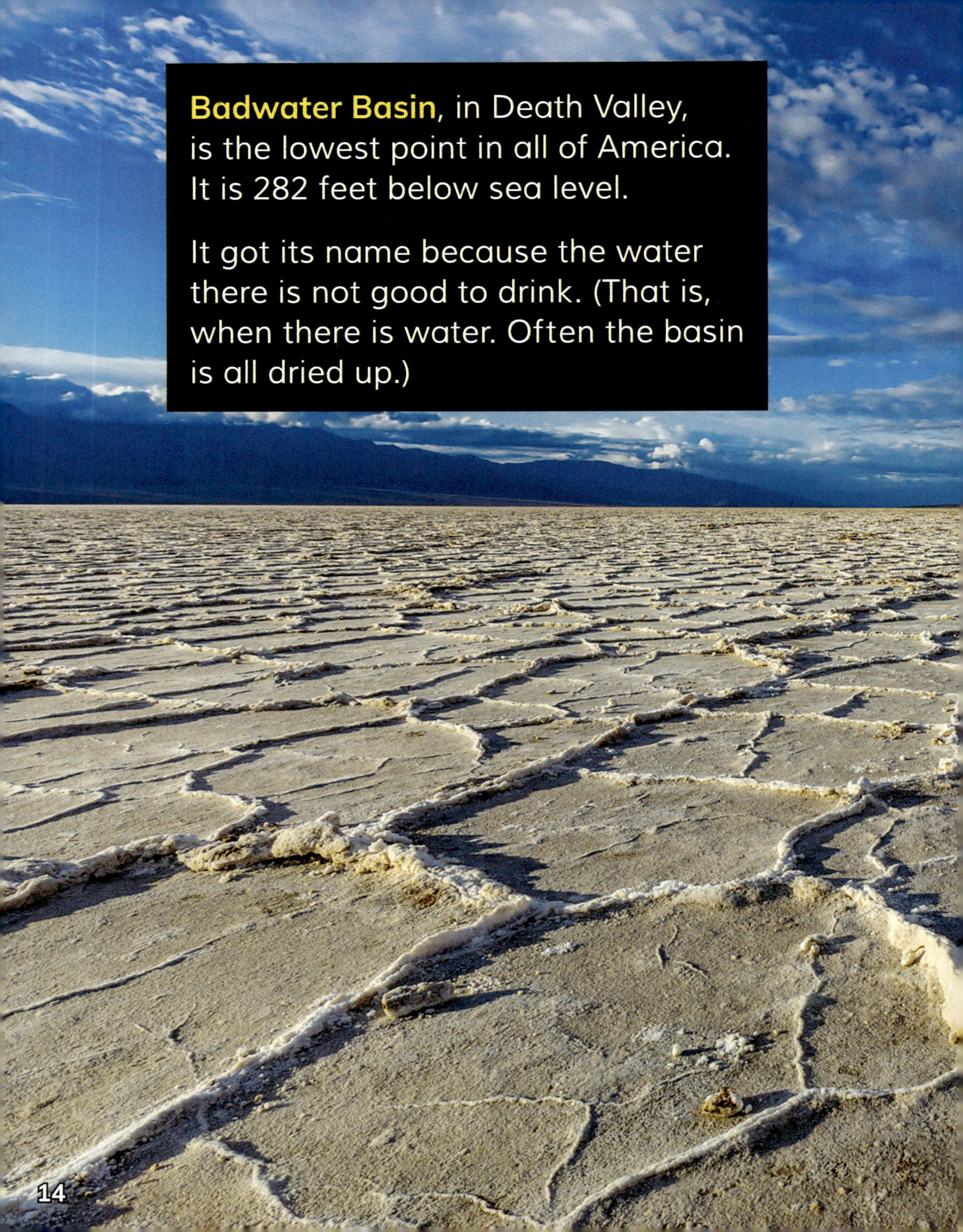

Badwater Basin, in Death Valley, is the lowest point in all of America. It is 282 feet below sea level.

It got its name because the water there is not good to drink. (That is, when there is water. Often the basin is all dried up.)

This is a fun fact – the lowest point on the planet **Mars** is called **Badwater Crater**.

It is named after Badwater Basin, because they are said to be similar.

Death Valley is renowned for its **sailing stones**, or sliding rocks.

These are boulders that seem to shift along the ground on their own, without help from animals, people or wind.

Experts are still investigating the phenomenon – so Death Valley still has some secrets!

Helen Keller

Written by
Jill Atkins

Illustrated by
Marie Muravski

Helen Keller finished speaking and sat down.

It had been a long speech, because she'd had a lot to say.

Yet her ears didn't hear the people clapping. Her eyes didn't see the people in the room.

In fact, she didn't see or hear anyone or anything.

Why? Well, we need to go right back to the start ...

Helen Keller was born in 1880 in Alabama.

Then, when she was still a toddler, she fell ill.

Helen's illness was an enigma. What was it?

Helen seemed to be getting better, but then she would shriek and scream. Mr. and Mrs. Keller were frantic. They just wanted her to be well.

Then, as time went on, it became crystal clear to them. Helen's eyes didn't see.

And not just that – her ears didn't hear. She was deaf.

The whole of their little girl's life was dark and soundless, with no sight or hearing.

In time, Helen made up signals to try to tell her mom and dad what she wanted.

Through her feet, she got to “see” people by the way their footsteps thudded on the ground.

Then, when Helen was seven, Ann Sullivan came to stay with the Kellers.

She had weak eyes too, so she understood some of Helen's problems.

Ann let Helen feel things. Then, with her finger, she spelled them on Helen's hand.

The first thing she tried was a doll.
D - O - L - L.

Ann Sullivan with Helen, when Helen was just 8.

At first, Helen didn't understand. Then, one day, Ann held Helen's hand under running water, then spelled W - A - T - E - R with her fingers.

Now Helen understood the link!

With Ann's help, Helen understood new things each day.

She had cards with embossed letters. She spelled things for herself.

With her hands on people's lips and throats, she found a way to "hear" people speaking.

In her teens, Helen and Ann left for New York. There, Helen attended establishments for the hard of hearing.

Soon Helen picked up how to speak – and from then on she gave many, many speeches.

For many years, Helen traveled far and wide with Ann. She gave speeches about how people without sight or hearing had rights. She spoke about all people having the same rights.

What she said in those speeches is still so important today.